NEW EDITION

YOUNG GIRLS
PUBERTY
& PERIOD
Book for Ages 8 -12

Natalia   Spark

Table of Contents

1

Are You Ready for Puberty?

Puberty is the period when you are growing from adolescence to becoming an adult.

Your body undergoes several changes as you grow bigger and stronger. Young girls typically begin to experience Puberty between 8 and 14 years of age. Girls usually start Puberty before boys do.

Puberty doesn't all happen at once—it's a slow process, and it takes several years in different stages. It might start at an early age or later in life. You will discover that everyone is unique and different.

You will find many materials helpful as you go through your period.

During Puberty, your body produces hormones, which are special chemicals that tell your body what to do. Those hormones instruct your body.

Some girls, experience Puberty at the age of 7. For example, breast buds are seen at an early stage. Also, they may become sore and tender as they grow.

Several Emotional Changes

Mood swings are a common aspect of adolescence.

Your emotions may get stronger and more intense during Puberty. You will experience more frequent mood changes.

Some girls get anxious, terrified, or angry for no apparent reason. You find them being sensitive and getting upset quickly.

What causes mood swings?

- Hormones
- Sleep deprivation
- The influence of others
- Expectations at school
- Family disagreements
- Fear, Stress, Anxiety, Self-consciousness

Hormones not only affect your child's physical appearance. They're responsible for changes on the inside!

Mood Swings and changes in your sleep cycles. These are essential in developing your own identity.

The nipple and the areola are raised over time. They will create a new mound on the breast. The breasts will be rounded at the end of Puberty, with only the nipples grown.

Pubic hair grows in a small area around the genitals. As the hair grows longer and darker, it becomes coarser.

You might find them on the thighs, too.

There is increased hair growth in the pubic area under the arms and on the legs. You can shave this hair.

Changing Body Shape

The first stage of breast development is a raised bump beneath your nipple.

This is known as a breast bud. One breast may develop more quickly than the other. Don't be concerned; the other breast will catch up. Your breasts may take several years to develop fully. As your breasts grow, you may want to start wearing a bra to feel more comfortable, and your mother can assist you in finding the right one for you.

Your body will begin to change. This includes your height and weight increase, but the hips may also widen. Fat accumulation in the buttocks, legs, and stomach may also occur. These are typical changes that occur during Puberty.

Weight gain

Her body size will increase, with her feet, arms, legs, and hands growing ahead of the rest of her body. Height and weight gain

Girls attain roughly 17 percent to 18 percent of their mature height around nine. If someone has told you that you are "all hands and feet," they are correct! Your limbs grow first, followed by your trunk. Most

Females grow the fastest six months before their first period begins (menarche).

You'll gain weight during adolescence; most girls do. You may find more body fat on your upper arms, thighs, and upper back. As the body grows, your hips become broader and your waist narrower.

Sweating

Teenagers may experience oily skin and excessive sweating as their puberty hormones rise. This is a normal part of development. It is critical to wash your face every day. Acne may form.

Young girls will menstruate every month. This begins when the body produces more hormones in preparation for reproduction. The body gradually begins to release eggs from the ovaries. This means that the adolescent girl is fertile. The uterine lining is shed through the vagina if the egg is not fertilised.

There's an improvement in critical thinking, allowing you to make plans and set long-term goals. It means more progress at a different rate, shaping your perspective on the world.

Looking Forward

Personal hygiene and taking care of the body make us feel better about ourselves and keep everyone healthy!

We could start brushing our teeth, hand washing, dressing in clean clothes, showering or bathing regularly.

Try brushing your teeth twice a day for around four minutes.

Brushing thoroughly removes plaque, which can result in cavities, toothache, gum disease, and even tooth loss!

It gives us nice fresh breath!

Your hands touch so many things daily.

Door handles, stair railings, and toilet flushers are all things we touch daily.

We pick up germs when we touch objects, which we might then spread by scratching our eyes, putting items in our mouths, and so on.

We may even unknowingly distribute them to our friends and family. Certain microbes can make us ill, transmitting everything from colds to Stomach problems (and much more).

Washing hands with clean, warm water and soap kills and disinfects germs.

Trim Your Nails

Keep your nails clean and nicely trimmed. Also, avoid biting them!

As we age and enter Puberty, it becomes vital to shower and bathe more frequently.

Both boys' and girl's bodies change during Puberty. Still, one of the most noticeable changes is that our sweat glands expand and generate more perspiration.

Clean Clothes

It is good to wear clean clothes. It would become dirty and smelly if we wore the same thing daily.

You do not have to wear new, clean clothes every day, but if you wear the same trousers to school for a few days, remove them immediately upon returning home, allowing them to air out!

Bring Your Underwear!

Your underwear conceals the areas that are prone to sweating.

This also applies to socks! Our feet are covered in sweat glands and can become sweaty and unpleasant due to the time we spend on our feet.

Change your socks and underwear daily! Also, place the soiled ones in the dirty washing basket rather than leaving them on your bedroom floor.

Keep Your Nose Clean.

Have you had a runny nose? We've all experienced it!

Tissues must be disposed of immediately or flushed down the toilet; do not share used tissues with others, and wash your hands after using a tissue.

2

Hormones and You?

Puberty is regulated by hormones, which influence your emotions and your body.

Your emotions may become stronger throughout puberty. You may experience mood swings.

You will experience sexual feelings and desires as a young girl growing up. You will be attracted to men, other girls, or both—sometimes called a crush. These emotions will decrease as you grow older. Puberty is perfectly normal.

Due to the mood swings, your emotions may be out of control. But you don't have to go through it alone.

Girls produce more testosterone than estrogen throughout their lives.

Estrogen is the hormone that causes visceral fat loss. Men gain visceral fat when they block estrogen, according to scientific evidence. They lose visceral fat when they stop blocking estrogen with aromatase inhibitors.

estrogen has gotten a "bad rap." Estrone is produced by your fat cells and is highly inflammatory. Estrone is to blame for all of the "issues" associated with estrogen. Estriol, Estradiol, and Estrone are the three types of estrogen. We tend to refer to them all as estrogen. Combining them all into one term is a mistake, and men and girls have suffered for a long time.

Take Note Of Your First Period.

The menstrual cycle begins on the first day of your previous period and stops on the first day of your next period.

Tracking your menstrual cycle means keeping track of when you menstruate and other period-related

facts. You might use a calendar and pen, or period-tracking applications have made the process easier.

If you prefer to count your period traditionally, mark the first day of bleeding with a slash or checkmark on a calendar.

The three to five days from the first indication of blood to the final appearance of blood is also used. A week that lasts between two days and a week

When your ovary does not produce an egg each month, your uterus grows, causing vaginal padding to be sent via your vagina. This is referred to as menstruation.

Hormones control

The amount of blood that flows out of your body is called your menstrual flow. You will have a stronger desire to eat.

Irregular periods occur when you have more or less menstrual blood than usual.

Within each cycle, the time changes.

Your period duration varies significantly.

Several reasons may cause this. The levels of progesterone and estrogen in your body vary. This is why Our Brain Requires Estrogen

This hormone has a significant impact on a variety of brain areas involved in functions such as:

Control of motors,

Learning,

Memory,

Defending against stroke and Alzheimer's disease

3

Stages of Girl Breast Development

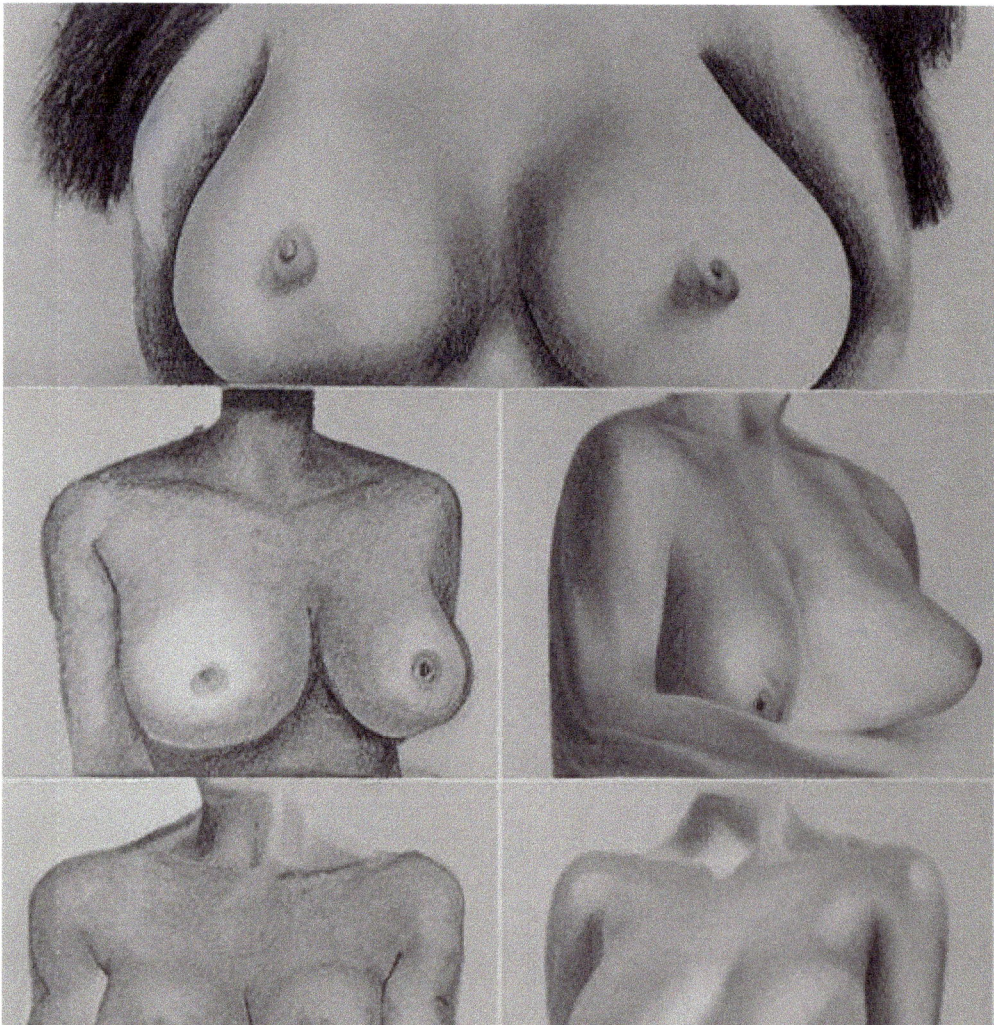

Stage one

Preteen. Only the nipple's tip is raised.

Stage two

Buds form, and the breast and nipple are raised. The areola (the dark skin area around the nipple) grows more prominent.

Stage three

Breasts are slightly larger and have glandular breast tissue.

Stage four

The areola and nipple rise to form a second mound above the rest of the breast.

Stage five

In an adult breast that has matured, Only the nipple is raised, and the breast becomes rounded.

Changes in breast texture happen during menstruation. These glands in the breast are enlarging in preparation for a possible pregnancy. If no pregnancy occurs, the breasts return to standard size. The cycle begins again when menstruation begins.

Questions about breast development

What causes breast pain?

There is evidence that suggests that breast enlargement may cause pain. Breast development is the result of the hormones estrogen and progesterone.

Your hormone levels rise throughout puberty. When this happens, your breasts will begin to grow. Hormonal factors account for fluctuations in the quantity of fluid in the breasts. As a

a consequence of this alteration, the breasts become sensitive or painful.

Don't you think my breasts will stay the same size?
Everyone is different. Breast size is not unusual, even if they vary a little or are of various cup sizes. Even while your breasts are still developing, you will quickly realize how common gender differences are

at this stage of life. Even if there is a major change in size, this is seldom significant.
Do I have breast cancer if I see a lump in my breast?
Although you will not always detect a lump due to the bumps you get, it is recommended that you do breast self-examinations (BSEs) to identify and remove any lumps you discover.

The milk ducts will start to develop glands when your menstruation begins. Secretion glands are sometimes referred to as "secreting glands.

Breast care

Here are a few tips to help you take care of your breasts.

1. Get a well-fitting bra: The first and most crucial step in breast care is selecting the proper bra. When purchasing one, make sure it is tight enough and fits you perfectly.
2. Should I wear a bra at night or not? This varies from person to person. Girls with smaller cup sizes can go without a bra at night, but those with a large bust must. This is because girls with heavy breasts find it difficult to move. After all, it falls on one side and causes discomfort while sleeping. If you must wear one, choose a fitting bra because it reduces breast movement and relieves pain.
3. Keep your breasts clean: When bathing, wash the area between the boobs and under the breasts, as these areas tend to sweat and increase the risk of infection.

1. **Avoid breast enhancement creams:** Many girls are unaware that the size of their breasts changes as they grow from adolescence to adulthood.

4

Your menstrual cycle

The average menstrual cycle lasts 28 days.

In the menstrual cycle, progesterone and estrogen induce menstruation. Here is how it works:

Your body has two ovaries, each containing a batch of eggs.

How does the menstrual cycle begin?

When blood flows out of your vagina, this is your first period, which occurs around the period of sexual development. Menstruation usually begins at twelve, although some people start later or earlier. Premenstrual symptoms (PMS) a few days before they occur.

A girl's menstrual cycle usually begins around two weeks before her period and lasts about one week. The typical cycle length for girls is 25 to 35 days, but it may range from 21 to 35.

Your menstrual cycle may begin and end around the same time as those you are closely related to, such as your sisters or mother.

Most girls have menstrual cycles that begin fourteen days before eggs leave the ovaries, but this does not mean everyone's bikes are the same. You can ovulate (release an egg) later or earlier in your cycle, depending on the phases of your menstrual cycle.

It starts on the first day of your menstruation. The lining of your uterus and blood flow exit your vagina at this time. If your period lasts for many weeks,

you are not pregnant. In pregnancy, the lining of the uterus does not develop, which means it disappears.

This happens about fourteen days after the start of your cycle, which is two weeks before your menstrual period. Hormones produced by an empty follicle in the ovary anticipate as the uterus is prepared to receive an egg fertilized.

DID YOU KNOW?

Girls may have short or long cycles, and having processes that run longer than thirty-five days is considered to have a lengthy cycle. Some individuals have a rotation of around twenty-eight days. Your menstrual cycle usually varies from month to month in length.

Menstrual fluid is believed to be shed at an average of one to six tablespoons during each period. Some things are brown or red, whereas others may be brown or red depending on how much liquid they have. As your menstrual cycle becomes heavier, you may need to change between pads or tampons more often.

- .Missed periods may mean that pregnancy is about to happen, although it's not always the case. Many other activities in your daily life may get in the way, which could disrupt your menstrual cycle timing.
- Periods, or PMS, prevent you from doing your regular activities.

You will feel very tense or sad when you receive your period.

Every 20 days or fewer, you will get your period,

Your Genital Organ

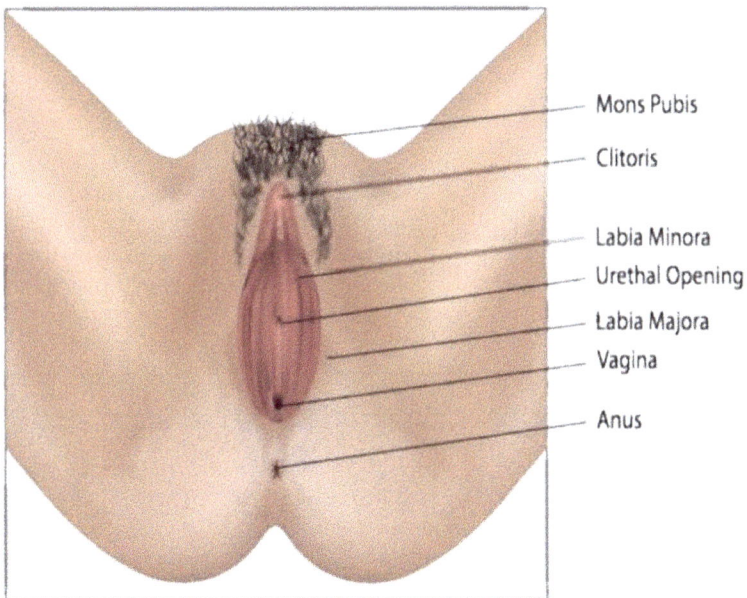

Mons Pubis

Clitoris

Labia Minora
Urethal Opening
Labia Majora
Vagina

Anus

5
Pads And Tampons

———

Menstrual products include pads, tampons, period underwear, and menstrual cups.

Pads, tampons, cups, and period underwear enable you to keep up your everyday life throughout your period. Menstrual inserts and tampons should be inserted into your genital organs.

It's a disposable, thin, flat fabric sheet placed onto the underwear. We have underwear with holes on each side or an elastic "arm," which helps prevent leakage or soiled clothing. This kind of pad includes non-recyclable components, so you only use them once before disposing of them. You may wash and reuse the pads made from fabric materials.

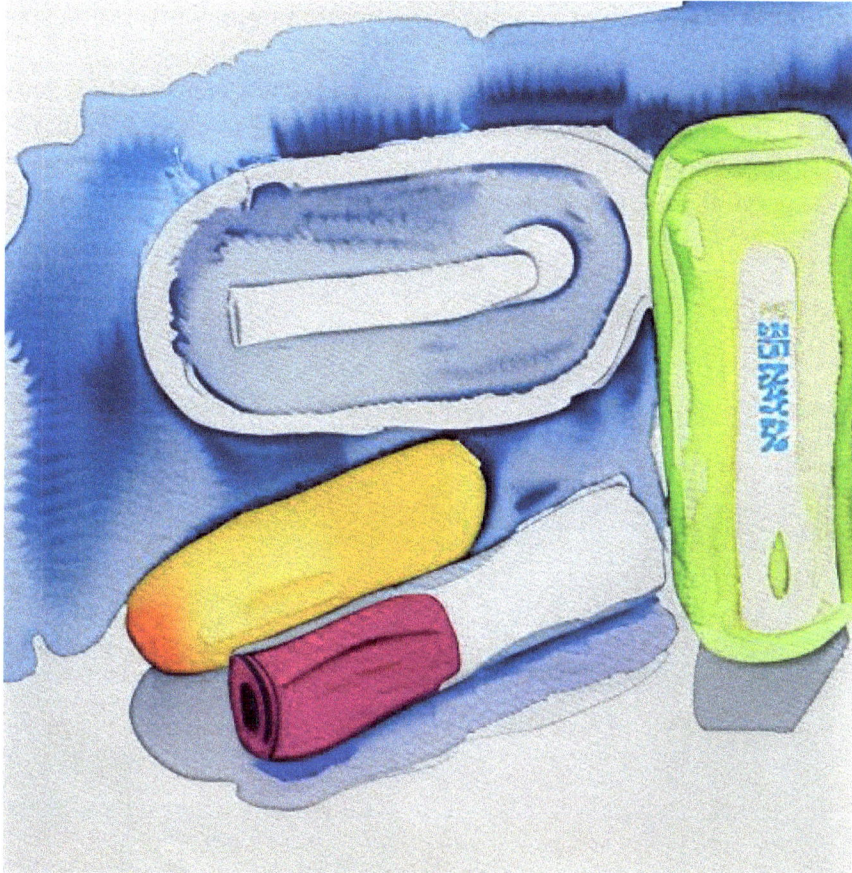

A Tampon is a cotton pad that is placed into the underwear.
While some cups and tampons may need to be properly placed for some, others may believe there are no cup or tampon arrangements. If you are

You may use cups and tampons to participate in sports activities while in the water.

Depending on the time of day, several items, such as pads or tampons, might be used during your menstrual cycle. A pant liner (a thin layer of protection) or period underwear using a cup or tampon as a backup protection method.

Engage in different activities, causing the menstrual pads to be uncomfortable or slip out of position. It would help if you put on a cup or tampon while doing sports or swimming.

Tampons vary in size, but they're easy to use if you're not menstruating heavily. Heavy bleeding pads are thicker. There are two types of writing to choose from, as long as you are more comfortable with one than the other.

Always change your pad at least every 12 hours or anytime it is saturated with blood.

Tampons should be used at any time.

Different tampons are available, including light, regular, and super-sized. If inserting a tampon with the smallest diameter takes you hours, use that one.

We have different types of tampons available; many come with simple step-by-step instructions. These may be tiny sticks made of plastic or cardboard that help you put the tampon in your vagina. You finger-tune them; therefore, there are no written instructions.

Wash you and get into a comfortable posture before inserting it. Sit in any of these positions if you don't place your other leg on the toilet, have your knees apart, or squat.

How to Insert a Tampon in Simple Steps

1. Employ visual aids.

Using a Diagram of the female reproductive system, note the angle of the vagina and how it slants towards the spine. Insert the tampon at angle 45.

a.   Locate the vaginal opening and (wash with soap first). Once you find the space and understand its anatomy (which can be the most challenging part), it is much easier to begin the process and avoid repeatedly poking yourself.

Be precise.

Start *Putting the tampon into your vagina using your finger or thumb.*

It feels better when you are relaxed. For easier insertion, use tampons with smooth edges. You can ask your mother or sister to assist you.

Throw out the application and wrapper in the trash when you are done with it.

You are to replace them every 4 to 8 hours. Even if you're on your period, you may use a tampon for the whole night and then change it in the morning.

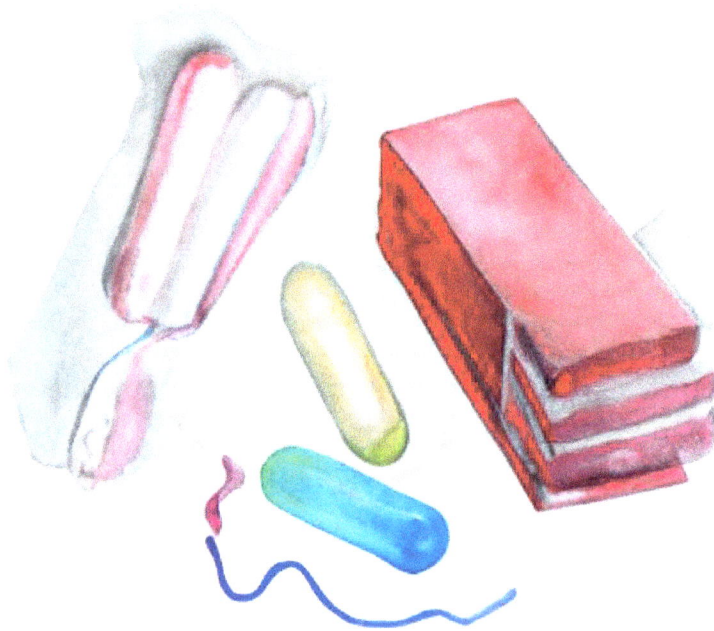

Tampons have a thread connected to the bottom of their vagina, which hangs out. They can be removed by pulling the rope up from the top. Removing your tampon while it is still wet and has absorbed as much menstrual blood as possible is simple.

Tampons may be folded and inserted. When this is done, the items are disposed of in the garbage.

To make the cup as thin as possible, squeeze it in your hand and use your fingers to enter it into the vagina. Follow the manufacturer's instructions to discover how to use the product and the best method to squeeze it.

The lowest part of your vagina holds up to six ounces of liquid. They should be positioned just above the cervix instead of in the vagina at the entrance to the uterus. If the cup is not set correctly, it might cause discomfort, especially if it isn't well-positioned.

Before placing the cup back into the sink, drain it carefully. You may choose to wash it at home or use the designated bathroom. Cups should be cleaned according to the cleaning instructions on the label.

Some cups are used just once and then discarded. Remove the wrapping sheet from the toilet paper-covered cups; pull it off and toss it in the garbage.

Period Pants

Period panties may be cleaned in the washing machine by using a detergent.

Period pants need to be changed, or you may use a tampon, pad, or menstrual cup to alleviate your flow.

Menstrual cramps

What are menstrual cramps, and why do they occur? During menstruation, the uterus experiences painful cramps that assist in the removal of menstrual fluid from the vagina.

Menstrual cramps cause discomfort in the lower abdomen. This might happen a few days before and continue throughout your period. Your flow tends to be at its heaviest in the first few days of your period.

6

The Teenage brain

The Teenage brain controls emotional swings and powerful neurochemical surges!

A huge manufacturing zone

The teenage brain moves from the explosive neurological growth of childhood to a change process that includes "synaptic pruning and myelination." Their brains are being remodelled as they progress from adolescence to adulthood. While this is necessary, neurological remodelling is messy, complex, taxing, and sometimes irritable.

They love Shorter, more frequent conversations. When discussing "big issues" like technology, substance abuse, sex and relationships, treating family members with respect, and even faith development. Teenagers respond better to an ongoing conversation than a "one and done." **The "emotional brain" vs. the "executive brain"**

During adolescence, the brain's emotional center comes online early and with ferocity. A teen's executive functioning—the ability to plan, make wise decisions, control impulses, and anticipate consequences— doesn't fully mature until he is 23 to 25. You may see flashes of brilliant executive functioning, moments when you think. Finally, he's got it, but those flashes could be followed by a stupid choice, such as spraying his biology teacher with a fire extinguisher on the last day of school.

Your emotional brain is large and powerful; you can model and teach them the "name it to tame it" principle. Adolescents are moving from the main reasoning to abstract thinking and expression.

Teenagers must understand the distinction between being angry and being hurt, being overwhelmed and becoming apathetic, and being unhappy and confused. When you know what your adolescent feels, you can help them work through it and toward godly self-control.

Teenagers are constantly observing and analyzing their surroundings. Their adolescent minds work nonstop, sifting through massive amounts of information from all walks of life. Because the teenage brain learns best through example and experience, how you act and think during this period is essential. In other words, God has given you an adult brain; your adolescent children rely on you to exercise more patience and wisdom than they do.

Why are parents unable to wake them up early in the morning? There is a biological rationale for this.

Sleep patterns change during adolescence in many mammals, such as baby rodents. Between puberty and the end of adolescence, the circadian clock programs them to sleep and wake up approximately 3 to 4 hours later than adults. This presents a problem,

they are still relatively sleep-deprived when you awaken them at 8 a.m.

It's something we should consider as a society and in educational programs, as chronic sleep deprivation impedes teenagers' ability to perform their primary function: attending school.

Sleep is essential for memory consolidation and learning. It's all about reestablishing synaptic connections, a chemically impaired process in a sleep-deprived brain.

7

Healthy Eating for Girls

Healthy nutrition should be taught to children early on in life, and eating well is essential to good habits.

Healthy feeding has several benefits.

Grains

Cereal grains may be turned into grain goods, including bread, pasta,

crackers, and chips. Whole wheat, brown rice, and oatmeal are among the

Options.

Vegetables.

Include a variety of veggies in your diet. Remember to include colorful veggies such as green, red, and orange, legumes (like peas and beans), and starchier vegetables.

Healthy Eating Facts

Poor nutrition from processed, salty, sugary, and fried foods contributes significantly to tooth decay and diseases such as diabetes, obesity, high blood pressure, high cholesterol, and cancer!

What appears to be a low-cost diet can quickly turn into years of medical bills for various health issues and medications.

In the long run, healthier options that cost a few extra pounds today will save you money. Isn't it fun to have a healthy body and lose weight?

Eating Healthy Foods Can Increase Your Happiness

An unhealthy diet is inextricably linked to mental health problems, specifically depression and anxiety.

Choosing foods such as bananas, fish, oats, nuts, and seeds will help you improve your mood and mental clarity. A happy body equals a happy mind, which equals more happy times!

Most junk foods have healthy Alternatives.

Try getting healthy alternatives to the most popular junk food dishes.

Once you've found a recipe you like, make a few batches and freeze them for future dinner indulgences.

Healthy Eating Can Help You Reverse Illnesses

Healthy eating can help reverse the effects of a diet disaster, just as unhealthy eating can cause serious health issues for your body.

Type 2 diabetes patients, for example, on a low-carb, high-protein diet, have been able to reverse their diabetes diagnosis and eliminate the need for insulin pills and shots.

Fruits

Anything in the fruit category must include at least a small amount. A wide variety of fruits may be found at grocery stores: whole fruits, chopped up, pureed fruits, and those in cans, in the freezer, or dried diary.

Milk products are part of this food category. Focusing on fat-free or low-fat goods, including those with extra calcium, is vital.

Protein.

Choose lower-fat meats and poultry, such as pork, chicken, and lean red meats. If you have trouble planning your meals, avoid the same proteins differently. Pick various fish, nuts, seeds, peas, and beans.

Nut oils are crucial to a healthy diet, even though they're not a food category. Animal fats should be avoided since they are complex and take a long time to break down.

 An overall healthy eating plan should include exercise and other types of daily physical activity.

8

Building Healthy Relationships

Relationships can be joyful and romantic, and sometimes, heartbreaks may occur. Choose your friends wisely.

Growing up affects your relationships and self-worth.

This causes a desire to be close to someone we are sexually attracted. It is expected during the puberty stages. Having feelings is a part of growing up. It's like falling in love for the first time.

What Makes a Healthy Relationship?

Respect for one another.

Does he respect you? Check to see if you like you for who you are. When you're not comfortable doing something, does he listen? In a relationship, respect means that one partner values the other and recognizes the other's boundaries.

Trust.

Does he trust you since he knows you'd never cheat on him? It's OK to feel jealousy occasionally; jealousy is a natural feeling. What is important is how a person reacts when they are envious. You can't have a good relationship if you don't trust each other.

Honesty.

It's difficult to trust someone who is dishonest

Support. Give your help always, not just at difficult times.

Fairness/equality.

Do you take turns picking which new movie to see? Do you spend as much time with your friends as you do in relationships? You'll notice if the balance needs to be corrected.

Separate   personalities.

When you start, you both have a life (family, friends, interests, hobbies, etc.) that shouldn't change. Neither of you should be forced to pretend to appreciate something you don't want, forego visiting your friends, or abandon hobbies you enjoy. Be free to pursue new interests or abilities, make new friends, and move on.

What Is an Unhealthy Relationship?

It is unhealthy when a relationship involves nasty, disrespectful, oppressive, or abusive behavior. Some people live in homes where their parents physically or emotionally abuse each other. Since Young people learn by observing and copying those around them, growing up in a toxic environment might badly affect them. Their relationships suffer as they can't treat people with compassion and respect.

Kindness and respect are vital qualities to have in any relationship.

.

Do you want me to stop doing something I enjoy?

When you're upset, do you ever lift your hand as if you want to hit me? Are you trying to make me go further than I want to go?

These aren't the only ones you should consider. Beware of people who try to control or make you feel horrible about yourself. That is not healthy as it could be harmful. Try to report an abusive friend to your parents.

Some teens misunderstand violence, possessiveness, or wrath as signs of love. Nobody deserves to be slapped, shoved, or forced to do something they don't want to do.

Both of you might seem perfect at first in any relationship, but that soon changes. If you try to keep the relationship going, it might eventually end badly. It's better to be separated or remain as friends than to stay in a relationship that hurts your personality.

Communication is essential to keeping healthy relationships.

2. Be there

Always listen. Try to comprehend their point of view while showing your interest. Ask about their experiences, emotions, and opinions.

Share information.

Sharing information promotes good relationships. Let others learn about you, but keep them from overwhelming them with too much personal information.

Be Trust Worthy. You might experience anxiety as a result of the change. Healthy Relationships allow change and growth.

4. Take care of yourself.

9

Consent and Boundaries

Consent is a vocal and positive statement of permission given to someone. It helps in understanding and respecting each other's boundaries.

Consent can be verbal or nonverbal. It is a secure form of consent. Here are some examples of verbal consent:

Verbal Consent

- "Yes"
- "That sounds fantastic."
- "That feels fantastic."
- "Let's do it more often."
- "I'd like to...," says the speaker.
- "It's a good feeling when..."
- "Could you please...?"
- "I'd like to keep doing this."
- "I'm having fun with this."

Non Verbal Consent

Nonverbal consent is another form of consent. There are nonverbal ways to express an evident willingness to engage in any activity. Nonverbal consent can be expressed in a variety of ways, including:

- Head nod
- Thumbs up
- Bringing someone closer
- Yes, I agree.
- Establishing direct eye contact
- Actively touching another person
- Beginning sexual activity

However, everyone's body language is different, and relying on it alone can cause problems. Rules About Consent:

- Both people have to want to do the activity. You can't force or trick someone into doing something they don't want to do.

- You need consent every time, even if you've done something before. Just because your friend hugged you once doesn't mean they want a hug every time. Always ask first.

- Consent can be taken back at any time. Even if someone said yes before, they can change their mind.

- Some things require a certain age to consent. For example, in Minnesota:

  - No one under 13 can consent to anything sexual

  - 13-16 year olds can only consent with partners less than 4 years older

  - Over 16 there are no age limit restrictions but you STILL need consent

Why Consent Matters:

- Respecting consent shows you care about others' feelings and boundaries. Doing something without consent hurts people.

- Many experience trauma, PTSD, emotional damage from non-consensual acts. This can impact them forever.

- Most assaults are by people the victim knows. Friends, dates, acquaintances, family members. Consent must be established in any relationship.

How To Practice Consent:

- Talk openly and clearly. Make sure all involved enthusiastically agree.

- Speak up if you don't want to do something, even if you agreed before.

- Check in as you go. Consent to one thing doesn't mean consent to more.

- Don't pressure others. Accept their boundaries without argument.

- Pay attention to nonverbal cues too. Look for enthusiasm and comfort, not just agreement.

- Use consent for all physical interactions, not just sex! Ask first for hugs, back pats, hand holding, etc.

Consent shows respect. Make sure all involved actively want to participate. Saying no is always okay. Speak up if you feel pressured or uncomfortable. Check in frequently. Prior consent doesn't equal current consent.

Setting Healthy Boundaries

Emotional and physical boundaries with others in our lives are essential to growing up.

Relationships. Boundaries help individuals know each other's needs and degrees of comfort. This establishes a foundation of respect, allowing both parties to feel secure and healthy in the relationship.

To establish healthy relationships, we must focus on expressing our limits as well as respecting the boundaries of others. Sometimes, this means developing appropriate coping mechanisms for our own emotions.

Here are some examples of good communication when it comes to establishing boundaries:

While spending quality time with your friends is also suitable for making time for yourself, your friends, and your family! It would be best if you had some alone time to yourself.

For example, *Can I come to the movie with you and Alex today?".* **You:"**

"Thank you. "I'll talk to you later."

You can choose what you are comfortable with and establish boundaries around what you want and don't want. Talking about comfort levels, likes and dislikes, and obtaining permission before doing anything is critical for establishing enjoyable sexual encounters for both individuals.

Communication is also required to develop respect, trust, and good relationships. More information may be found in our Consent section!

Body Safety Rules:

The five body safety rules are a great place to start when teaching young girls about body safety.

Sample Rules You Can Set:

My body belongs to me.

My body is under my control. If I want to avoid being hugged, kissed, or touched. I can say "NO!" to a touch I don't want.

Our body parts have proper names.

And everyone has them.

We shouldn't look into each other's private parts, touch them, or play games with them.

The areas of our bodies covered by a swimming suit and hidden from view are known as private parts.

I love keeping it Secret, especially concerning my private parts. There is a distinction to be made between good and harmful secrets. People enjoy good secrets, such as when your parent asks you to keep your grandma's birthday present a secret so she can be surprised. It's OK if you keep that information hidden.

It's called a lousy secret when someone touches us unsafely or perplexingly. They may ask you to keep it a secret, and they may be delightful or offer us gifts in exchange. That is a poor secret to keep, and it is not acceptable to do so.

My Boundaries

I have five individuals I can talk to if I'm upset, afraid, or need to discuss body safety! If someone violates a body safety guideline, I must report them until someone comes to my aid. I will only be in trouble if I tell you when it happens.

For Parents

We should teach young girls that it's never their fault if someone touches them unwantedly. It's also a good idea to talk about how an adult who looks after children might need to touch a private part to keep them healthy and clean, such as when they go to the doctor, take a bath, or change a diaper.

When someone isn't respecting my Boundaries, what do I do?

Discuss it with them. Tell them they need to stop. You are crossing your boundaries, and this is not acceptable. Speak to them when it's safe about it.

If it's not safe, or if they continue to violate your boundaries and you've spoken to them about it, it's an unhealthy relationship.

10

Becoming Better in School

Doing your homework and assignments is necessary to improve your grades. However, you'd be amazed at how many students skip lessons, leave tasks unfinished, or wait until the deadline before completing them. Here, we give some tips to help improve your school grades.

Eat Early

Breakfast is the most important meal of the day. It has been proven to enhance attention and memory (both of which are vital skills needed for learning). Eating breakfast at school has been shown to improve school attendance and math results in children from low-income Households.

Practice the Growth Mindset - Students with a growth mindset do well in school, accomplish their future objectives, and improve their overall grades.

Put Your Phone Away in Class

Distracted by your phone splits your attention, making concentration and learning harder. Being on your phone has several unfavorable psychological effects. It has been proven that students who spend more time on their phones reading emails, Facebook, and texting receive worse marks, independent of gender or prior academic performance, in a study that won an award for 'stating the obvious.

Find out Why You Are Anxious

Spend a few minutes writing down what makes you anxious.

Use your free Time–

Students who spend more time playing video games and less time on homework/reading do poorly on tests. According to a study, students who spent an additional two hours before a screen received 18 fewer points. Students who spent an extra hour doing homework or reading each day got more points.

Get a Good Night's Sleep –

Not getting enough sleep may affect memory, focus, mood, creativity, health, and concentration. This has been shown to have a detrimental impact on your math and language grades.

11

Online Safety for Girls

The internet has become an integral part of our daily lives!

Sometimes, you feel as though you couldn't live without it! These guidelines will assist you in remaining secure online and avoiding damage.

1. Use strong Passwords

They are intended to safeguard your information, so make sure they are strong passwords containing letters, numbers, and symbols that no one else can guess. They should not be shared with others and should be changed frequently. Do not use the same password for all of your accounts.

2. Use the Privacy Settings

You can control who sees what information about you or your location by using the privacy settings on social media and apps. Only individuals you know in real life should be able to see your information.

Personal information

Don't give out personal information like your name, email, phone number, address, or school name to individuals you don't know. It would help if you ensured this information is not accessible to everyone.

4. **Profiles**

Make sure no one can get too much about you from the material in your profile, bio, or the backdrop of your profile picture. Remember that others may store or share everything you write on your friend's list.

Visit only safe websites.

A padlock icon in the browser address bar indicates that a website is safe. Before entering, check for sensitive information, such as payment or address data. If it isn't, don't utilize the website.

12

Skin Care Tips

Skin layers

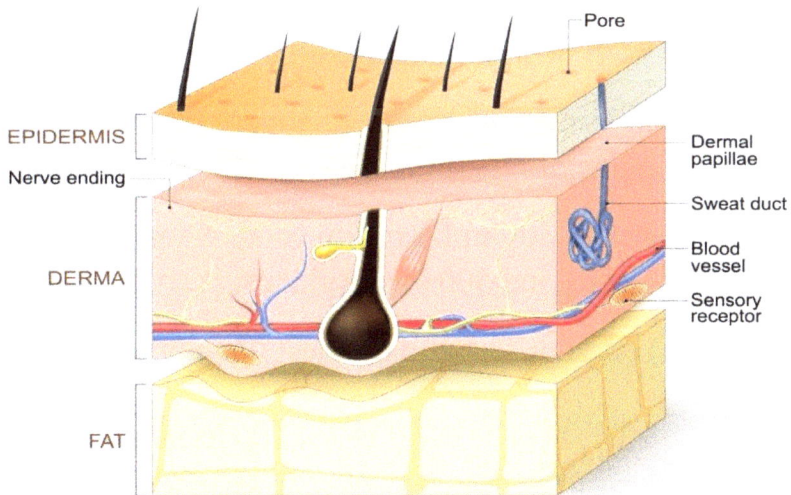

EPIDERMIS

Nerve ending

DERMA

FAT

Pore

Dermal
papillae

Sweat duct

Blood
vessel

Sensory
receptor

Skin issues arise as a result of hormonal changes in your body. The production of oil, also known as sebum, causes a noticeable difference in your skin. Excessive oil and sweat accumulation keeps dirt within your skin cells. As a result, the pores become clogged, and acne breakouts occur.

- **Around 15% of your body weight is made up of skin.**

The average adult's skin measures approximately 21 square feet, weighs 9 pounds and contains over 11 miles of blood vessels.

A typical person has approximately 300 million skin cells. A square inch of skin contains about 19 million cells and 300 sweat glands.

Your skin is thickest (1.4mm) on your feet and thinnest on your eyelids (0.2mm).

Every 28 days, the skin regenerates.

Your skin constantly sheds dead cells at approximately 30,000 to 40,000 per minute! That's almost 9 pounds per year!

Good skincare should begin in your teens when your body changes rapidly. It keeps your skin in good condition and prevents premature ageing from causing problems in the future.

We should establish an effective skincare routine.

Here are a few easy Steps to Having Healthy skin:

1. Use A Gentle Cleanser

Wash your face with a cleanser appropriate for your skin type to keep your skin from drying out. Use gentle, circular motions to reach every inch of your face.

Avoid using soap (unless specifically designed for washing your face), as it can irritate your pores and cause acne and pimples.

1. Use a Skin Moisturized

Use a moisturizer twice a day to keep your skin supple and hydrated and prevent premature fine lines and wrinkles.

If you have oily skin, use a lightweight, oil-free moisturizer to avoid clogging. If your skin is prone to acne, use gel-based moisturizers.

A good moisturizer sunscreen protects the skin from the sun's rays.

a.   Treat Acne

While acne can occur at any age, teens will likely experience acne breakouts during puberty. Hormonal changes cause them.

Face washes, creams, foams, and gels containing benzoyl peroxide are chemical substances helpful in treating acne.

a.   Protect the skin from too many Sunrays.

Some vital sun safety tips are as follows:

Limit your time in the sun, especially between 10 a.m. and 2 p.m., when the sun's rays are strongest.

Wear sun-protective gear, such as long-sleeved shirts, slacks, sunglasses, and broad-brimmed hats.

 Reapply sunscreen every two hours at the absolute least and more frequently

if you're sweating or hopping in and out of the water.

 Wear long-sleeved shirts and wide-brimmed hats when going outside to protect your skin from the sun's rays.

a.   Look After Your Lips

Before going to bed, apply lip balm.

Apply some cream to a baby toothbrush, wet your lips, and then gently scrub for a minute with the brush. Apply lip balm and wash it.

1. Apply Hand Cream

If you have dry hands, apply some hand cream. Applying it regularly, including in the morning and before bed, will provide the necessary moisture. Just be careful not to use too much cream, as this will make your hands oily and slippery.

1. Avoid frequently touching your face.

Touching your face could spread oil, dirt, and bacteria that can lead to blackheads!

Also, refrain from picking at your pimples! This can spread infection, damage skin tissue, and cause additional inflammation.

Use gentle yet effective spot treatments to clear your pores of acne-causing bacteria. One of the best acne treatments for teenagers is benzoyl peroxide. Before making any decisions, you should consult with a dermatologist.

Always wash your face twice a day with warm water. [4] It aids in dirt removal while preserving your skin's natural hydrating oils.

a.   Follow a Good sleep Routine.

While you sleep, your skin rejuvenates itself. Before bed, cleanse your face, remove all traces of dirt and makeup, and apply moisturizer, lip balm, and hand cream.

13

Building your self-esteem

Being self-confident can take some time; young girls with low self-esteem, self-love, and acceptance are more likely they grow into confident, capable girls.

Signs of low esteem

A girl with low self-esteem is likely to have negative thoughts about their worth and value as a person. Some general indicators that your child has low self-esteem are:

üavoiding new experiences and failing to seize opportunities

feeling unloved and unwanted while blaming others for their errors

ü-inability to cope with normal levels of frustration

ü-negative self-talk and comparisons to others; fear of failure or embarrassment; difficulty making new friends üLow motivation and interest, inability to accept compliments and mixed feelings of anxiety or stress

There are things you can do to help your child develop positive self-esteem. Still, it's also important to remember that adolescent self-esteem develops and changes rapidly. Suppose your child does not immediately exhibit signs of positive self-esteem. In that case, it does not necessarily imply that you are doing something incorrectly!

5 Ways to Develop Self-Esteem:

1. Develop a grateful attitude.

A gratitude journal can assist young girls in capturing and expressing these feelings. Also, journaling promotes self-confidence, improves communication skills, and elicits mindfulness – all of which can help girls build self-esteem. "What are you grateful for today?" is one prompt that can help you get started. Or "Write a letter thanking yourself for all the wonderful things you've done."

Practice self-affirmation.

Positive affirmations in the bathroom are excellent ways to boost your self-esteem. Write these words like "I am beautiful, I am worthy, and I am enough" somewhere visible daily, especially on sticky notes.

3. Be a Volunteer.

As a young girl, I remember volunteering at community concession stands within my religious community and in various volunteer activities through Girl Scouts with my mother. It not only made me feel good and

 It taught me the value of giving back and helped me create positive memories with her that I still have today.

4. Develop your mindfulness skills.

Yoga and meditation benefit the body, mind, and soul and can be a gateway to self-discovery, acceptance, and love. Mindfulness encourages people to breathe and concentrate on letting go of negative thoughts. If yoga is not a good fit, practice mindfulness meditation in your morning routine. These are deliberate and meaningful steps toward self-love.

5. Be Creative.

Being creative is a powerful way to express self-love and self-care. Try something simple like cooking dinner or baking a new dessert. Try new tastes and flavors. You will learn valuable life skills and improve your cooking skills. The possibilities are endless. Gardening, music, creative writing, and even board games can all stimulate the creative mind.

14

Growing up can be fun.

I know you're growing up and with a changing body, you enjoy the attention of guys, but for the sake of your young reputation, you should keep your clothes clean.

Appreciate your hair right and find a way to style your hair in its natural state.

Family is important

Make sure you're forming strong bonds with your family. Put less emphasis on having a boyfriend that you miss out on quality girl time. The bonds you form with your family when you're young will last a lifetime, and trust me; you'll need their love and support on more than one occasion.

Romantic relationships are cute and fun.

Respect your parents. They have paid for everything you're wearing right now, as well as the device you're using to read this article. They care about you more than you'll ever realize, and being mean to them isn't the way to show them how grateful you are for everything they do.

Every year of school is another building block to add to what you learned.

The previous year, so keep up, or you'll need to catch up. Plus, no matter where you end up, your intelligence will always get you far.

Boys mature at a slower rate than girls. Also, your body will draw attention to you.

As you are growing up, you will become better.

What An Amazing Journey

Get the Boys Puberty Book Too

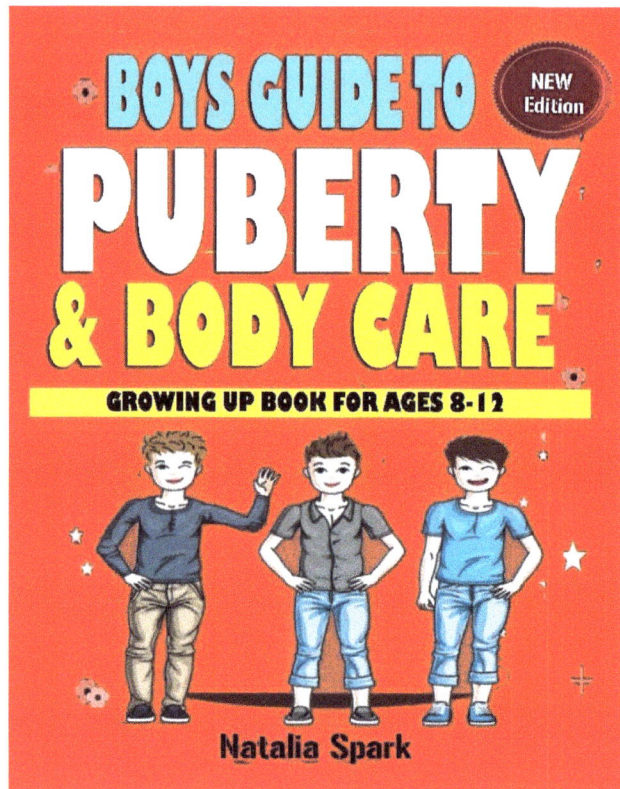

BOYS GUIDE TO
PUBERTY
& BODY CARE

NEW Edition

GROWING UP BOOK FOR AGES 8-12

Natalia Spark

www.ingramcontent.com/pod-product-compliance
Ingram Content Group UK Ltd.
Pitfield, Milton Keynes, MK11 3LW, UK
UKHW052038250825
7566UKWH00012B/951

9 789789 919079